Shiva Moon

poems

Maxine Silverman

[signature] March 18, 2018

For Terry Gross, with admiration, Maxine

Ben Yehuda Press
Teaneck, New Jersey

Published by Ben Yehuda Press
122 Ayers Court #1B
Teaneck, NJ 07666

http://www.BenYehudaPress.com

ISBN13 978-1-934730-59-1

19 18 17 / 10 9 8 7 6 5 4 3 2 1   20171008

Also by Maxine Silverman

Palimpsest
Transport of the Aim
Red Delicious (in Desire Path)
Survival Song
52 Ways of Looking

for my sisters

in memory of our father
Abe Silverman
(3/5/1917 – 12/16/1999)

and for his grandchildren

Contents

Preface

On December 22, 1999, the full moon coincided with the winter solstice and lunar perigee for the first time in 133 years, resulting in an unusually beautiful and brilliant celestial display.

A month later on January 20, 2000, a total lunar eclipse occurred over the Americas and western Europe. Totality was particularly dramatic over North America where the Red Moon could be observed high overhead on that cold, clear night.

Also significant, the Winter Hexagon was easily visible to the naked eye, as well as a number of other stars and deep-sky objects normally not visible because of the moon's brightness.

In this context, family, friends and I sat shiva for my father. The poems in *Shiva Moon* trace the year of saying Kaddish for him.

North Star

Look,
my father murmured, *how*
my hand shimmers.

Palsy drew light to him
until it filled his body,
illuminating the long bones
curving around his heart and breath,
drawing shadow limbs
to radiant joints,
until he limned for all the world
some constellation,
my father
telling the dark between stars.

○

Almost six feet tall, 129 pounds, my father
may remind you of certain haunting photographs,
Jews stumbling from the gauntlet
of bloodthirst and indifference,
wandering among the skeletal remains
of their lives.

My father is worn to the bone,
one full year
grinding another,
the flesh of his belly collapsing on old scars.

Breath drawn in their wake   stars

The Boys Sleep Late

the way children do in summer, deeply, one breath after another,
no school, another and the morning's still cool.
On the porch I watch vines twine up the rail, wait for the blossoming
I know will come. Maybe I read *Open Closed Open*,
sip raspberry-laced tea, maybe no one calls from the road.

Already I walked with Alice: look
Regina's corn and corn flowers, Bob Boreman's tomatoes,
not ripe yet, not so many since Carol died,
too late for impatiens?, tickets for starlight jazz, how
sweetly our new hazzan sings.

Plant a dozen flowering vinca, their white blooms
crisp as midsummer linen.
So far so good, Dog and I agree. We want them to keep on
sleeping so we can glide on cool green metal
near a rail of morning glories not yet blooming, hope
no one calls, no sister crying,
"You better come home. Dad keeps falling." I am home.
I live on this porch
sorting seeds, collecting thoughts, words pulled one by one
stop time awhile and
not thinking at all really I sing *Ease his way, Lord,*
sort of to the tune "Kumbayah,"
a procession in my voice, clear rain, deep green and
white with the center red.

My boys shamble out,
slamming the screen. Day begins where the last one ends. "Momma,
I'm hungry, Momma, make him stop, Momma, can we swim?"
Ease his way, undertone so they won't ask, "Momma,
What're you singing, why?"

Dream in a New Place

Last night I dreamed something woke me,
comforters rustling when he turned, a sigh.
I watched myself hurry to his room
through a tunnel, easy by now
though I never lived there. As a child

visiting a new place I'd check before sleep
(slippers right by the bed) for the best way out
in case of fire. This night

I could see my father sitting on the edge
of his bed, about to rise—one last kiss, thirsty,
or needing to pee again as old men will.
His arms felt all bone in a loose skin sack, no flesh
on his back either beneath his thin travel robe,
but warm. "Here, Daddy," I smile, "Let me help."
"It's okay, honey, I can do it." but he couldn't,
not even in a dream.

What I Learned So Far

When Ellen says my poems these days seem one seamless Kaddish,
I hear she understands the six months
before my father died were raw keen k'riah.

How June's visit home I see his death
forming in the air he breathes.

Why every evening I call him
until there's nothing left to say,
until all that remains—the sheer
pleasure of his company.

Elul. He weakens before my eyes,
no shofar blast required.

        Tishrei. We daven
repetitions to dwell in meaning: who shall live
and who shall die, who in the fullness of years

        We cross into wilderness, a new year,
pillar of fire before us, the old, the weak, the infirm
to the rear, Amalek plucking them one death
at a time.

        Reservations for December.
My father says, "Come right now." and I do.

A way is made.
Gathered to his people,
a story old as time.

How It Was

Rick and Ann offered. I said no
don't straighten him,
I want my sisters to see
how it was,

left hand tucked under his cheek,
right hand curled below his chin,
one breath a little ragged,
the next a little more

so I wasn't sure and glanced up to Ann
  yes she thought that was it.

Yesterday
I reminded him—
his parents, brother and sisters,
certain friends,
how he remembered them
we would remember him.

I may have said the Sh'ma. I know
I sang "Danny Boy," his favorite,
and one he didn't know,
anyway would hear the tune.

A little later his breath
began to gutter more

or less all night. This morning
I was holding his hand and held his hand
until I went to call my sisters
to tell them how it was.

Leviticus 18:7

how else to wash the exhausted body,
to marvel at breath's tangible beauty,

to murmur psalms all night long

Maxine Silverman

Journey Cake

We fill his breast pocket.
Not what he needs,
what we need to give
for the rest of our journey.

"Here," said Connie,
"a clean hanky
he won't find in the next world
either"

and on the plain wood
four red roses,

on the roses
earth,
three shovelfuls each,

on our shoulders
sun

as we turn to leave him
under a bare-limbed tree.

Shiva Moon

O Thou
  rare gathering of unbearable loveliness,
solstice, full moon, lunar perigee,

winter's first day and shiva's fourth,
  midpoint of the first week's mourning
in a year of grief

keen-edged and round.

                    O

The first night I rose
in the minyan
I took care of each vowel,
every syllable.

Second night
I almost stumbled
from my low bench.

Third night
I do not rise alone.
  Joe in the third month of mourning
his mother,
  Barry's eleventh for his father
(soon to unveil the headstone),
  Esther steadying herself
for her husband's third yahrzeit.

The almost familiar words
  clump in my throat,
          the Aramaic thickens.

Nearer than ever,
   shimmering before my eyes
      my father's face

full, bright, infrangible
   love, nightly the minyan gathers
      momentum, intangible, memory's eruv.

○

Old Farmer reports to the minyan:

*The moon will appear about 19% brighter
and 9% larger than your normal full moon
thanks to a celestial confluence.*

Moonspun-gold closer to Earth
than usual,
closer than a full moon's whirled
since 1930,
while Earth nears her orbit's point
closest to the sun,
both at winter solstice.

But, warns Sky & 'Scope editor K. Beatty,
   Some people might not notice.
   You may want to keep your headlights on.

○

A Found Poem

In his second drawer lay an oversized envelope
I mailed from Lit, Sweden a quarter century ago
for Chanukah, his gift—

      vivid watercolor map signed by hands outlining
      the space Countenance shone through,

      brown-inked Baedeker of the village,

      "Neighborly," poem-portraits in purple,

      and this dream still green:

      Little sister and I live in my room at Storhogen near Lit.
      Outside my door, in the hallway, is a worn carved bench.
      We come out and see you seated on this bench, Daddy.
      Another figure, in black, broods in a far corner,
      turned, not really part of the scene. Your face glows

      some other-world light. You had been blind, but no more.
      We come closer. I begin to cry and stroke your cheek,
      "Miracle, miracle."
                      "No miracle,"
      your graceful reply, "when you are faithful you can see."

                    O

        Old Farmer cites a full moon brighter
            another longest night
              Earth and her moon
          spun slightly nearer the sun,
        degrees of brightness brighter
      than this medallion set in jet-black.

            Maxine Silverman

A Small Craft Advisory

His bad spells prepared us, rehearsals
we called them, dry runs, a test
of the emergency broadcast system

and all us good farmers came running
with our hoes and scythes,

yet Daddy's death surprised me.
Shiva, and the Nazis bust up my dream.
I know it's real this time
though I wake before the bullets
splatter brains across the quilt.

Father, aged, infirm, invalid, still
the world's not safe without him.

Years back if the S.S. crashed a poem
at once I'd rub them out.
What were they doing in a ballad about Pearl,
a river flowing beneath my hometown,
in lyric or landscapes,
no matter how free the verse?

Not skilled enough to control
the language swirling, I selected
Nazis to the left. Everyone else to the right.

"You can't help but write more than one at a time,"
a workshop teacher explained.
"That's how imagination works, a magnet
pulling any and all with the least trace of irony."
Her advice: don't edit, don't censor.
Writing down the page,
she solved the problem. Cunning, efficient girl
underlined each subject a different color—
    peat bog and related stuff: ochre,

blood red for coal miners striking,
black holes, well, you get the picture—

parsing, she saw patterns, combined each color
into a separate poem.   Imagine color coding Nazis.

She wasn't wrong and she isn't right.
Listen,
  my father died in his own bed,
  morphine to ease his way,
  his daughter holding his hand.
Blam! they storm in any way, looting dreams,
stomping, shouting, shooting.

Nazis aren't subconscious anything.
Generations after Auschwitz, they still have their way
with us, show up when you least expect.   That is the poem.
The rest—commentary.

Carrots

A boy bends to his task.
His shoulders round with exertion
under his flannel shirt festooned with stegosaurus,
a blunt serrated pumpkin carver
chosen for the bright plastic handle
to match his carrots.

Now and then Owen glances toward the stove.
"Enough carrots?" She can decide, his mother
knows this much.
He rearranges the stubby tubers and resumes slicing,
his entire self absorbed in making orange circles.
Round upon round drop into the measuring cup,
half full. Half empty? Both, at once,
he knows this absolutely,

he wants to stay here helping with dinner.
Windows frost over, the rich steam
of ginger, and garlic from the summer garden,
clouding the panes.
How he bears down, his undivided attention,
lets you know he believes here
is the way through the dark tunnel of days.

Shloshim Eclipse

Mourning's 30th day
it dawns on me. Without him
is the rest of my life.

Where have I been
that I didn't know?
I saw death coming,
no place to swerve.

Slowly, the passenger of a car struck head on,
painstakingly, on hands and knees
in the intersection, gathers shards one by one.

Is this glittering cold *glass*, is it *ice*,
prism, *gem*, who could they shield
from wind or rain?

○

Metaphors, young Owen once explained,
are okay for people who don't know
what they want to say, who need
to tap meaning on its shoulder, you're it,
who conjure a car wreck when there was none,

when there was: watching

○

A total lunar eclipse is gradual,
time released, like some capsules,
certain photographs, shock.

The fact of Absence,
that knowledge,
accrues.

○

I am trying to say *gratitude*,
to be this daughter, raised in that same town,
living now by water flowing both ways
with one particular man, these very sons.

Older, I say irony becomes its own eruv,
a boundary nothing can be carried across,
what is meant by *self limiting*

while my father's absence goes on and on.

○

from www.homeplanet.com:

*The first total lunar eclipse since September '86
kicks off a busy eclipse year in America. Unlike
solar eclipses, this celestial event is risk-free
and requires no special equipment.*

Thursday, 10:01, day 33, the ruse begins.
Our own moon eluding us,
Earth's umbra
slides across solar brilliance

reflected.
        Moon slivers
deeper into Earth's deep central shadow.

Over the years some observers report narrow bands
of color in the transition zone between umbra and
penumbra . . .

O

Totality,
the Moon glows rouge
in a clearing of altocumulus

backlit ghostly snow shadows.
En umbra, in its time,
the Moon emerges silvery, shimmering

appears whole once more
in the firmament.

O

Visible in his eliptical presence
stars outshone no matter how clear the night

Aldebaran,
Rigel,
Procyon,
Pollux and Castor,
Sirius,
Capella

Our Little Joke

Whatever you call what you can't touch
that holds you here, I call our Father
in his Absence,
one reference shy of irreverence,
one joke short of comfort.

His words I hear from my own lips
often enough, expressions so peculiar
they could be fingerprints.

No snapshot will suffice, no virtual dad for me,
I want to see *him* again. Obliging, he shows up
with my dream, in profile, backlit. I have to guess
his expression, but it's Daddy all right,
his warm pj smell, shoulders boney now,
a tad hunched as he sat at the end
of his bed, and yes,
he helloed his custom-made endearment.

It was the night after the day I knew would come,
one of those cliches of mourning.
5 p.m., I dialed
the way I'd phone every evening,

knowing a day will come when I'd give anything
to ask, "Is this the party to whom I'm speaking?"
and we'd grin.

What I Learned So Far (2)

Chana Beila taught: the Hebrew of Job
is so obscure, the meaning is lost
among translations, especially the ending
scholars find ambiguous.

I asked, "Maybe not even God knows
why we suffer?"
                She answered,
"What we're left with is the poetry.
Sometimes in the spaces between text
we find the Teaching."

○

Immediately I phoned Lee,
hoping poetry would help with her thesis
on the meaning of suffering in the AIDS colony
of Newark.

○

After Havdalah, after Kaddish for his mother,
Rav Yochanan taught: "Kaddish
was not originally a mourner's prayer.
After study the rabbis and their students
sang Kaddish d' Rabbanan.
Death is never mentioned,
only God's sovereignty, God's will. Maybe
that's the association to death and mourning."

In seven instructions
Kaddish teaches

God's name should be
blessed, praised, honored, extolled, glorified
adored and exalted
                    beyond our ability to praise.

But how, when we are wrapped in grief,
and how, when entering or leaving rooms
we touch loss—lips to fingertips,
when we daven our swaying reminds us
of being rocked, rocking, how?

"If we hold a memory of our beloved
(an afternoon fishing, a favorite song)
it is possible to praise.

Try, that's all I ask,
let me know."

Early Morning Lambs

New lambs gambol in winter's brand-new brawn.
Willows glisten around Spook Hollow Pond,
a bright frozen cascade of tender green.
In my garden, early blooming ice sculptures gleam
at first light. Might as well marvel
at winter's last gasp. Black ice in April—
who could predict, did Old Farmer forecast
this latest high jinx of mourning's vast
oh surely unreliable weather?
Stepping from the porch, hugging my wool sweater,

I walk with Alice as planned—no lambasting
the regular uncertainty lamb blasting
me—half-orphaned translator, pilgrim child,
my father's Kaddish, at last reconciled.
   And if you believe that, I have a bridge
across a gorge, over a ridge
to my mother's house in a foggy place
knowing can't go. She can't recall his face,
no name for his absence, for him, for her.
I'm her Kaddish too, then, a wing, a prayer.

Sugar

In truth he was a champion of trees,
transplanting pin oaks marked for the ax
from Sacajawea Scout Camp to our backyard.
After work he tended them and drank beer in their shade.
One evening Dad and Stanley Miller
(who helped dig the holes) finished another Bud

and called Mom to confirm the new star
they spied. "Dream on," she crowed, "Fools,
don't you know antennas when you see one gleam?"

The fool she married planted vegetables, his garden
a block square, gooseberries, strawberries,
seven blossoming trees.

Legendary grew the six sugar maples, one for each of us,
one for our brown-sugar mutt,
                                in no time Midrashic,
higher than the house,
            so you'll understand why, when we learned
he'd bought extra plots in Zion Graveyard, five in fact,
we decide to plant trees there, and you'll know why,
when I open the envelope
offering free sugar maples,
two with each purchase,
I order dogwood, pin oak, apple, plum.

Called Back

Memorial Day, Jersey shore, midnight
I wake in a guest room.
From the living room my sons talk in an undertone.
Midway, in the hall between rooms, I pause,
listen to their deepening voice rise and break apart
with laughter, lull and whisper. Feet cold,
needing to pee, I am the girl again
wading in a dark inland sea, hearing my parents'
low voices review the day,
decide what happened, what it means.
> *Oh speak a little louder*
> *I am ready now to hear*
They were not my parents after all—
just themselves together, husband and wife
in their own house, resting in soft grey chairs,
one on each side of the brass lamp,
book and evening paper open in their laps—
or if it happened I woke later
they would already lie deep in their darkened room,
side by side in twin beds.
> *I can't make out quite*
> *what the boys are saying*
to each other on the fold-out couch, broad raft
they drift on, their dog nestled between.

They will be all right. They will be friends, by and by
will help one another build their mother and their father
each a narrow craft. Oh can you also hear the dark
soughing waves, the hushed voices
of another time, from another place,
> *not now, not yet*
Their father wakes. "Come back to bed."
> *In a minute. I'll be right there*

Maxine Silverman

We Dream of a Green Rowboat, Amber Lake

As a boy her father rowed across the lake for mail,
    to Bud & Bailey's for eggs, news, and milk.
Across the lake she sees his childhood home
    and hers, behind it oak, maple, sumac ascending,
rise after brilliant rise to the tree line, a mountain's way
    of saying *where the air thins only memory of trees*
and the wish for trees grow.

    At first his shoulders burned a little rowing back,
then the oars' dip and pull were no more work than breathing.
    The oar locks' scrape reminds her a little of geese aunking,
the flare of oars their wings rising over the lake, her arms aching,
    of stories her father told when she was young. So she keeps
on rowing, rows and rows as if her life depends on rowing,
    a green rowboat, eggs and milk.

Driving Lesson

At twilight and first rainfall
take care.
These moments
bring peril to the road—

  on again brights, off again light,

    creatures dart from the edge of things,

    rain slicks the blacktop grime—

then darkness and the road even out.

What lessons did your father teach?
You heed a man whose brakes snap
in the Rockies, late afternoon sun
aiming fire at the windshield,

who steers the green Chevy between cliff face and gorge,

his girls playing Slap Jack in the back, only tin rail and him
between them and thin-wild air,

coasting to a stop, loosens his grip to flag some help,
orders pan fried steak at Tucker's All Night.

Mostly brakes hold, and luck. All the same, when light falls
or rain, I look for him.

What I Learned So Far (3)

Sherilyn stopped her sweeping to teach me.
"Maxine, I have a story. You know in Antigua
we had no snow. Well, yesterday with my boys,
there is no school because of this snow. I send Akim
and Malik out to play. I look, there's Malik lying,
struggling with his arms and legs. 'Akim, Akim,
oh my God, something is wrong with your brother.'

Well, don't you know Malik is laughing, 'Ma,
I'm making an angel! Don't you ever make an angel
when you was a girl?'
                                    Isn't that something,
Maxine, isn't he too much that Malik?"

What I Learned So Far (4)

When I phone Bea for the meaning
of the names, she knew Malik right off
and how to find Akim.
                      Then she asked
could I help her? She already consulted
Cornell Extension. What the woman suggested—
Bea was to shut her flue, cover her hearth.
the bird should fly to the light—
hadn't worked to shoo the bird from her chimney.

I knew this much . . .
she mustn't light a fire thinking it might urge him up.
What if the bird is hurt?
                    And then I remember
this story *tsistsistas* badger told the children: *I teach*
in prisons too. Once in a workshop of hard timers,
the men and I
heard a bird. I had just read them Vallejo's poem
"After a Long Time Traveling." We realized the bird
we were hearing was trapped in the heating duct.
We all began to cry.
                I called for the guards.
Then we wrote some poems. What more could we do?

Maxine Silverman

Witness Protection Program

Who would guess on the plain near Zo'ar a witness stands disguised,
a watchtower the taste of tears glowing on the moonlit shore of a dead sea?

Who would know the mountains of blessing and doom are really safehouses?
From Mt. Gerizim honey flows through the green town Brucha.
On the barren slopes of Ebal, boulders are rolled for windswept huts,
rest stops along the way.

In garden courtyards, by fountains, in dank alleys, near gates
where dappled ponies drowse, through tunnels blasted through granite,
by fires where drifters warm themselves, by still waters,
the witness takes note.
With her forefinger she traces a dusty map, nods and rubs it out,
scratches passwords into soap with her fingernail until by heart she can recall,
verbatim, what she saw and all she heard.

Deep in Amber Lake lie some who saw too much,
woke too late for escape, so the story goes, whose tears fell from blind eyes,
little stone tears, stories left graveside and mums, stones, crocus, stones
on stone marking a trail.

If I tell you Amber was changed from Ambra,
that the meaning of this native word is obscure,
that perhaps, the current owner of Bud & Bailey's store claims,
Ambra meant something about trout transported in skins from far north
and rinsed here in this deep-cold to keep the flesh fresh,
that only elder locals know the lake's name refers to anything older
than the color of certain algae,
you will also know Ambra is not lost at all, but safe under the surface of
things.

O my father, almost a year has waxed and waned
since I watched at your deathbed, each full moon I sit shiva again,
in memory holding your hand as in fact I did that morning.

Last Shabbat I woke in darkness with this sentence

formed whole from an unremembered dream,
  Let me join the Witness Protection Program.
A rest from remembering, that's all I need,
say the month between the eleventh of Kaddish
and his first yahrzeit.

Some day I will go underground for good, for now
a little joke gives respite, a poem safe haven—
  kauneonga: white water, *callicoon*: wild turkey—
what I know, all I saw and heard.

Early Morning Rabbit, Late June

Last night's rain lifts as fog by the river,
rises in dawn turgid with peony
and mock orange. A small black dog leads me
toward Hook Mountain along the familiar route,
the same sweet houses dreaming. Morning
glories furl tight yet I know, circling back,
their blue fists will extend open-handed
on white fences, so dependably the planet slues
on her reliable axis, late June.

By the tumbling stone wall,
one trickster, brown ears radar straight,
bolts—trading camouflage for sanctuary
and the understory.

All tendons and intention, the black dog springs,
yelping, after the early morning rabbit.
How the earth finds over and over
ways to break through the morning fog,
called back
sticking his cold nose into my palm
begging to be noticed, to be loved, to be
on the way
home.

The Month of Elul

(after reading *Open Closed Open*, Yehuda Amichai's last book)

In my garden every spring, before a single seed, I plant the trellis, a staff of white
spokes flared, a fan opened, a hand reaching. Trellis leans lightly on porch rail,
white post and trellis bound by green tangles of morning glory and moonflower.

This morning the vines stagger under the weight of six mammoth moonflowers,
razzle-dazzle blazing-white trumpets still trembling from their last dark crescendo.
Now the moonflowers are shriveling, collapsing on their own ivory throats,
white-hot sun putting them away for the day. I don't think of pajamas
hanging on a closet hook or from my father's withered frame,
but of the cornet my son yearned for, well used, suspended
in the pawn shop window on London's Portabello Road,
curiously not for sale.
Despair brought this Salvation Army clarion to the three bright spheres
proclaiming *here, the last dreams you cling to, here*.
The proprietor grew to love the engraved gleaming horn,
dented slightly and bent at the bell's slender throat, hung it for a sign.
Well, I think,

the mind is a funny thing, memory its best joke and then I do think of my father,
driving somewhere in the family car, happening past a graveyard,
asking each time "How many people dead in there?" and each time answering,
"All of them, they're just dying to get in."

O

When does late summer steal away to early fall, late autumn ease into early winter?
I'm looking for the border, the guard asleep at his post. Why, I wonder,
isn't the little wind a sufficiency,
slipping through your fingers as day gives way to night,
that mysterious span we call evening? Exactitude, precise and keen,

was not what we looked for in the brown Dodge or green Chevy
when my father drove past graveyards,

Maxine Silverman

my sisters and I in the back seat, our mother beside him.
Those days I was content to wait for his answer, a punch line we remembered
as soon as we heard it, laughing more for the pleasure of remembering than wit.
He knew the answer, we were together, as I recall, in laughter and love.
Maybe the Dodge was green and the Chevy brown.
If I think of it, I'll ask them, my sisters.

O

Now it matters if summer's late or autumn early.
In the days since I first planted a garden, in the encompassing embrace
gardens require of their tender, the joy learned from my father tending his,
I scan the moon, gauge the rain, gather bouquets or harvest
what good soil produces and deer somehow miss.

Now I care about names botanical and common, the Doctrine of Signatures,
all manner of wives' tales and husbanding lore. Now that I'm middle-aged

(probably older than my parents driving somewhere in a brown Dodge),
I find these points of reference useful, comforting

(though how do you find middle with only one point fixed?).
All we know for sure—how many dead in a graveyard.

O

And we understand all graveside visitors will reside there one day,
dearly beloved,
receiving guests of their own.

O

Torah teaches: the head of the year, the same certain day in the endless round

of days, begins the end of days. So we pray, "Return us as in days of old, give us
hearts of wisdom, more mercy than justice that we may hope where innocence knelt,
Old-What's-Your-Name, our Father our King, teach us to number our days
driving by graveyards telling jokes.

○

Jacob, whose name recalls my father's father, looks over my shoulder, confirms
all I have written here, except the cornet he craved was, in fact, a baritone horn,
like the one he plays in Band IV, held on his lap to his chest, practicing for the days
of holding a child to his heart, the only music at the end of the day that counts.

○

Last year the morning glories and moonflowers grew beyond the trellis, their vines
swaying in thin air, groping for purchase to extend their reach. So I strung twine
from nails in the porch rail, around the trellis, through the wrought iron rack

we stack firewood in. Web for growing, wood ablaze with flowers, morning, moon,
I don't think of my father so much in his grave. Tending—then,
and when I'm kind to kids or trees—
or when some foolishness springs from my lips and we laugh.

Thus is his good name bound up with lovingkindness, his soul with wisecracking fun.
Day by day I love him more, less than I will, moonflowers drawing close as morning
glories flare, blossoms among firewood waiting for the flame.

○

Elul. Soul-splitting every day, in the thirteenth month of the lunar year, clarion
shofar detonated three by three times three *tekiah shevarim-teruah tekiah*

He walks up the center stairs to the ark (Where oh where is the cord to pull him back from holy encounters with death, from uttering the Unspeakable Name wrong, vowels hidden, vows annulled?). Standing beneath the ner tamid, God's live coal-smoldering Eye, my son looks like any recruit in sandals and shorts,

sunbronzed, muscular thighs, sunbright hair catching light along his limbs
and at his throat,
embroidered skullcap over flesh and bone
where the birth pulse beat.
Recites two benedictions, may the Source of Blessings bless us, already sanctified,
commanded, bless us granted, sustained, enabled to reach this day. Amen. Amen.

Now is he ba'al tekiah, Joshua at Jericho, blower of shofars, master of rending air,
Ezekiel the Zealous, ready, prepared to awaken sinners and resurrect the dead.

Brings a long translucent curling ram's horn, the color of staunched blood, to his lips.
Waits for the rabbi to pronounce, in an undertone, quiet with awe,

> *tekiah   shevarim-teruah   tekiah*
> *tekiah   shevarim-teruah   tekiah*
> *tekiah   shevarim-teruah   tekiah*

At the sharp blasts even angels, accustomed to joyful noise, cover their ears,
malachim are roused and congregations murmur standing before the open Ark.

> *tekiah   shevarim   tekiah*
> *tekiah   shevarim   tekiah*
> *tekiah   shevarim   tekiah*

Only Mt. Moriah could withstand this raw bleating, these resounding ragged cries.
She's heard them all before.

> *tekiah   teruah   tekiah gadolah*

Is any cell in any body still locked, any soul unreturned?

O

And God? Surely God won't turn a deaf ear.

Yaakov ben Meira   *Avram ben Meira*
                    Yaakov v'Avram b'nei Meira

O

Moonflowers droop, withered by the midday glare.
No water can revive them. Morning glories revel in that same shining,
oh Heavenly Blues.

From the Front Porch I Survey My Garden

After a week's absence (inconstant sun where I retreated to the mountains, constant showers in the valley where we live) I tell you my garden is dizzy with growth. Vivid blue hydrangeas bow, grounded with their own sizeable blossoms glittering with rain—morning glory vines crisscross trellis to trellis, search the air for purchase—cucumber vines sprawl in every direction, leaves hairy, elephantine.

Planted and mulched a few days before my departure, a hedge of clethra sweetens the morning air. Below shrubbery, along the stone wall, wild flowers zig-zag—blazing coreopsis, beaded smart weed, a creeping vine with dainty blue flowers, sun flowers of staggered heights, bee balm—and every window box spills over —crimson petunias, purple-black sweet potato vines, pansies of all hues, brazen nasturtium, dame's rocket.

A chipper scarlet pair lights on stewartia whose slender armature is visible now the bleeding heart has been pruned. The stewartia, still a sapling after all, quivers under their double heft. Grass too wet for mowing, the cardinals join some sparrows for earth-rinsed worms. Rain, the earth is besotted with it.

Amid riotous blooming, grief, creamy and delicate, flutters dreamily, feasting on the abundance I have planted. My father likes to stay in touch.

What I Learned So Far (5)

Umbra and penumbra,
perigee, when to plant a tree,
Kaddish deRabbanan,

Aldebaran . . . Castor, Pollux
. . . Capella

in other words, the winter hexagon,
one of those fabrications
for plumbing the fathoms of night.

Specialized bodies of knowledge,
disciplines,
require their own language,

grief's aleph bet,
the jargon of mourning,
a grammar of loss and longing
in the context of love v'kavanah.

I learned   palimpsest is richer
than irony to convey shades
of meaning,
                    k'riah or any visible sign
of mourning are not worn on Sabbath,
                    pentimento may explain
faces of people "not there,"
                    zachor—a life's work.

Putting the Garden to Bed

We live in different time zones, my sisters in Central,
I where the sun sets earlier the same sky.
There too, time flies.

The year rounds toward our father's yahrzeit.
In secular standard time and lunar,
we mark the days.

Putting the garden to bed for winter I think about borders
and beds blooming, their leaves taking in whatever light for days
and days on end, of plants feeding on light gathered
and stored in roots, tubers, corms and bulbs
until the whole earth is a squirrel with bulging cheeks.
At least this hemisphere.
On the other side earth ripens, lush, voluptuous
ovary opening purple, scarlet, gold, for every pollinator around,
clamoring unabashed and brazen, Take me
oh take me to your table your bodouir to your breast.

Wind picks up, the afternoon darkening.
Hurry. Mulch around the summer sweet,
smooth the cover of oak leaves where crocus and iris
will resume their habit of blooming.
Hands growing numb and still there's burning bush
and buddeleia . . . Sedalia, where he lies buried—

you name it—maples in fall, apples in spring, tomatoes
in summer, Juicy Fruit offered to some kid, the way my son holds his fork,
evening light and morning's, a particular phase of the moon,
certain acts of kindness—
anything at all might bring him to mind.

Right now I happen to be putting the garden to bed,
watering the shrubs, coiling the hose, going in to call my sisters,
Remember how   and   *Remember the time*,
what passes for hope among bare branches,
cold comfort in other words.

Flying Stand-by, and other stories

> No words, only supreme/joy in being visited
> —Alicia Susman Ostriker, "What You Want"

See, Daddy, I almost smile,
somewhere between Nyack and Newark,
 I did listen.
You would know Richard felt worse than I—
losing the way, driving fast too late
for the flight home. You would grin
as I say aloud to the man steering furiously,
 No harm done, my dad would say,
I'm going nowhere fast.

The sky opens.
Somehow I manage not to cry
though my joy for your visit wells up.
Richard would think I weep for my ticket unscanned,
skywalk wheeled away, flight attendants seated for take off
while we circle the Garden State
with no clue.

 We'll wait, you and I, to unveil your stone
 Better late than you know what and fly stand-by.

In the eleven months my father
has lain next to his sisters—
who lie next to their parents
encircled by iron, a gate
with Hebrew words arching
whose meaning requires decoding,
letters broken or lost, no vowels—

stories, a flood of them have come my way.
An empty basin, all I've done is receive them, wait
shaken, grateful for the next and the next,
and read what I am given by the malachim.

A year to get the point. What joins us—delight
in making stories from the *stuff* that happens,
and these stories, his gift to me, pour in
so long as I tell them to you
and you.

What I Learned So Far (6)

Dress for the weather.
Go out into fallen snow.
Gather a handful and roll it along.
Repeat. Stack them in a circle three snowballs high.
Place a candle in the center of the circle.
At sunset light the wick.

A Mourner's Prayer

How fortunate to buy a white candle,
to know when to strike the match,
shovel dirt and hear it thud
on the lid, to reminisce
over photographs (to have photographs)
and fold his clothes for those less fortunate.

How luxurious to say Kaddish for one person,
letting grief resonate, deep bell tone
thrumming deeper and round.

O Love, reverberate, ricochet.
Loss and longing, lash out.

    She knows precisely who
she weeps for, leaving a stone on his stone
near the stone his father and mother share.

Welcome, Grief,
resident alien, *baruch haba.*
           Memory
will count Father in the minyan
of a daughter's heart.
                Year after year
how privileged to light the candle.
    Most fortunate daughter thanks her father,
tear after tear.

December

Flame even as breath

Snow falling on first yahrzeit

Flickering keepsafe

Early morning walk

from within dark wind and snow

delicate chiming

Maxine Silverman

One Small Regret

That apple core he offered—how I wish
I'd simply put my pen down and thanked him.
I wish I'd gone straight away for the spade.

When tender seedlings braved our bracing air,
I wish I'd tended them as I watched him
tend his seven blossoming trees, as he
watched over pin oaks and sugar maples.

Winter deer would not strip the saplings' skin.
My children would never wrestle too near.
Three Levitical years fruit could ripen,
and fall. Only now would I pick apples,

slice and pile them in a crust, with nutmeg
and a squeeze of lemon juice. Only then
would I reach for my pen, only then.

What I Learned So Far (7)

Night.
A tribe gathers around fire.
Someone begins a nigun.

Low Bench

I return to the low bench.

Kaddish on the bright cusp of solace

year after illumined year.

Maxine Silverman

Afterword

I write about you all the time, I said aloud.
Every time I say "I," it refers to you.
                    — Louise Gluck
                    "Visitors from Abroad"

Maxine Silverman

Orbits and Occultations

My father has two yahrzeits,
one secular standard time, fixed, the other lunar,
waxes and wanes and waxes.
Every 19th circumvolution they coincide.

December 16, the perigee, the point nearest his death,
rounds the days' order.

7 Tevet, death's moon, circles 12/16, one year earlier,
later, closer, farther, unhinged
from solstice or dayside. Diasporadic, I am
at a loss to know what time it is
or what is time that death shifts it so
and fathoms the deep chasms of space.

And now, the third year out,
my soul recalls his out of Time.
By the speed of Kaddish we realign.

There was sundown
was daybreak   a fourth year.

Orbits and Occultations (2)

Sky Watch: Week of December 23

Old Farmer consoles,
If you missed the occultation last month,
rise and shine, 3:30 a.m.

Fix your sight well east of the almost full Moon.
Trace the two illuminati moving east to west.
Hour by seeming lunar breadth per hour,
Moon gains on Saturn

until Saturn disappears, red rings passing
behind the Moon's dark edge,
emerging 29 minutes later, a virtual half hour,
on Moon's bright edge, dark-bright dissolving into dawn
easing into morning another year.

Night Light

After we buried our father, the moon came nearest
earth's center, resplendent in its wholeness,
most expansive night of all other nights,
the Shiva Moon.

Every full moon since, I report the news
as if visiting his far away grave, my night words
the stones laid on his stone, homely words, rough,
unburnished, steadfast. I say how I miss him still,
how his grandsons grew, how they fare.
If no one else is walking her dog,
I might sing.

Notes

Traditional Jewish mourning begins with ritual washing of the body. Once prepared for burial, the body is never unattended; members of the community stay in the room to recite psalms or other prayers. At graveside, by shoveling three scoops of dirt onto the casket (traditionally plain wood), mourners help with burial, setting in motion a sequence of grieving periods which remove family members from daily routine and gradually return them to normal activities. Shiva, the most intense mourning period, lasts seven days. Remaining at home to be comforted by visitors, mourners sit on low benches. Each evening of shiva there is a brief home service requiring a minyan, ten adult Jews, so Kaddish may be said. For Shloshim, the next three less intense weeks, family mourners return to jobs and most other duties. Depending on one's relationship to the deceased, responsibilities vary. Adult children say Kaddish for a parent for eleven months, ideally every day, stopping after the eleventh month and resuming on the twelveth for the yahrzeit (the anniversary of the death). Yahrzeit is observed each year thereafter by lighting a candle and saying Kaddish.

Except where noted, terms are Hebrew and standard transliteration is used. All definitions of Hebrew words or terminology are taken from *A Glossary of Jewish Life* by Kerry M. Olitzky and Ronald H. Isaacs.

Akim – masculine name meaning "God will provide."
Aramaic – ancient Semitic language Kaddish is written in, similar to Hebrew.
ba'al tekiah – master shofar blower
baruch haba – literally "blessed are they who come," used as a welcome greeting
bima – raised platform in synagogue sanctuary where Torah may be read

brucha – blessing, name of modern Israeli town on slope of Mt. Gerizim

daven – pray

Days of Awe – refers to the ten days of intense reflection between Rosh Hashanah and Yom Kippur

Elul – the month in the Hebrew calendar that usually corresponds to August in the secular calendar, takes on the character of repentance before Rosh Hashanah (new year)and the fast of Yom Kippur

eruv – ritual boundary line

HaMakom – literally "the Place," one of the names of God, also refers to a tombstone

hazzan – cantor, clergy who leads prayer in synagogue services

Heavenly Blues – a common variety of morning glory

kaddish – prayer traditionally associated with mourning

kavanah – prayerful intention

kipa – prayer cap, in Yiddish: yarmulka

kriah – ritual rending of garments

lamb blast – seasonal opposite of "Indian summer," a wintery storm in spring that threatens newborn lambs and tender shoots

Maheakanituk – Mahican name for the Hudson River meaning "water that flows both ways"

malachim – divine messengers, sometimes translated as angels

Malik – name meaning "prince"

Meira – feminine Hebrew name meaning "light"

Midrash – commentary on Torah often in the form of stories

minyan – quorum of 10 adult Jews needed to say Kaddish

mountains of blessing and doom – Deuteronomy 27, 12-13, after Israelites cross into Canaan, God orders the priests to extol blessings (if they obey Torah) from Mt. Gerizim or doom (if they do not) from Mt. Ebal

Mt. Moriah – mountain identified as the place where Abraham prepared to sacrifice his son Isaac.

nefesh – breath/soul

ner tamid – literally eternal light, seed-red light hanging in the sanctuary before the ark where Torahs are kept as a reminder of the omnipresence of God

nigun – wordless melody used as meditation or transition between parts of prayer service

Old-What's-Your-Name – reference to one of the Hebrew names
for God which was only uttered on Yom Kippur by the high priest
in the holiest place of The Temple in Jerusalem, now the exact
pronunciation is not known

seed-red light – ner tamid

Sh'ma – Jewish "watchword," prayer "Hear O Israel, the Lord your
God is One."

shevarim – double note blast on the shofar.

shevarim-teruah – combination of shofar blasts shevarim and
terurah

shloshim – literally 30, less intense period of mourning after shiva

shofar – ram's horn, historically used to herald freedom and
assemble the community for war or public occasions, sounded at
Mt. Sinai and during the month of Elul

shul – Yiddish, meaning synagogue

tekiah – shofar blast, 2 notes, the first longer than the second

tekiah gadolah – the great tekiah, prolonged second note

terurah – "broken" shofar blast, alarm-like sound consisting of nine
rapid notes blown on the shofar

Tishrei – month in Hebrew calendar when Rosh Hashanah and
Yom Kippur occur, usually coinciding with September in the
secular calendar

Torah – Hebrew Bible, the Five Books of Moses, literal translation:
the Teaching

tsistsistas – literally "the people," traditional name Cheyenne call
themselves

Yaacov v' Avram b'nei Meira – Jacob and Avram, sons of Meira.
In Jewish tradition children are usually identified by their father's
name, except when asking for healing or safety of the child when
their mother's name is used, tradition that in certain critical or dire
situations God is more likely to listen to a mother's plea.

yahrzeit – anniversary of a death, Kaddish recited each year

zachor – to remember

Zo'ar – town near Sodom where Lot hid after his wife turned into a
pillar of salt

Acknowledgements

Thanks to Ellen Kahn Froncek for permission to use her handmade paper as the image for cover art. The paper was made from iris pulp and indigo at The Women's Studio Workshop in Rosendale, NY.

Artist's Note: "One of the pleasures of hand making paper is that one can still sense the life force in the materials. And so it is with Maxine's poems. They, too, are still alive with the emotion and experience of a life deeply felt."
—Ellen Kahn Froncek

"One Small Regret" is for Howard, Don and Tineke, with love.

"Early Morning Lambs" is in memory of my mother, Jeanne Lane Silverman (9/25/1918 – 10/23/2004).

"Driving Lesson" was previously published in the anthology *Rough Places Plain*. Thanks to the editor, Margot Wizansky, for permission to reprint the poem.

More poetry from
Ben Yehuda Press

is

heretical Jewish blessings and poems

we who
desire

Poems after the Torah

Sue Swartz

Words
for
Blessing
the World

Poems in Hebrew and English

סדר ברכות את העולם

Herbert J. Levine

is

heretical Jewish blessings and poems

Yaakov Moshe

"The best mystical poets tell it like it really is. Funny, touching, sobering, and uplifting, the poems of Is remind us that we are an oh-so-ephemeral part of the cosmic nothing, barely glimpsing the nature of reality under our own skins. Yet these poems also remind us of our deepest experiences of being alive as individual embodied beings. Is invites us into stillness and emptiness, but also into laughter and love."
—**Rabbi Dr. Jill Hammer**, author of *The Hebrew Priestess*

"*is* is a very compelling book, full of Judaic Zen-like Koans and whispers that invite the reader to ponder what is, what isn't, and what might yet be."
—**Lesléa Newman**, author of *Heather Has Two Mommies* and *A Letter to Harvey Milk*

"These so-Jewish and so-Zennish poems are perfect prayers for the holy congregation of postmodern exiles, they who are eternally unsettled yet lovingly warmed by the flames of their unrequited yearning."
—**Avraham Leader**, founder of the Leader Minyan

Yaakov Moshe

On entering another's place of worship

Light which shines through forms,
Reality of many names,
as we enter this place of holiness,
grant us insight to see you,
grant us balance of mind
to love our own and another's forms
polyamorously for You.

As we uphold ancient precepts
by men scared of idolatry,
guard us from idolatry in our hearts,
which mistake form for Light.

As no form can contain you,
your vastness encompasses multitudes.
As your will is untranslatable,
your essence is beyond concept.
Remain with us, Holy One,
so we may honor our path
and You.

Outing God

Stop hiding
Enough war already
Enough hunting

I love you
but your energies can get filtered so much sometimes

Sadness, delusion are bad enough
But ignorance causing cruelty causing devastation.
Oy.

neither optimism
nor pessimism
is justified

god holds cancer
and love
and humiliation
and dandelions
and devastation
and compassion
and rifles
and peacefulness

At my hour of greatest joy,
I do not want too much exuberance,
because there is suffering,
and people are inflicting it
needlessly.

Yaakov Moshe

This is not only about Poland.
It is in the simplest of cruelties. Including mine!
And this is not about piety or holier-than-thou.
Just,
clarity
in the midst
of joy.
Remembering now,
as I hope to bring memory
to darkness.

This game of hide-and-seek:
you play too well.

So, yes to ecstasy
But enough already —
if you play this game much better
I don't know who or what you'll play with.

The truth is not out there
It's in here
Waiting for you to help it
Come out

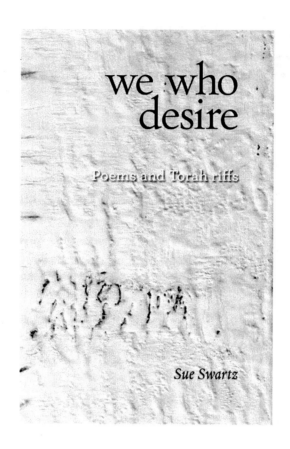

we who
desire

Poems and Torah riffs

Sue Swartz

"Sue Swartz does magnificent acrobatics with the Torah in *We Who Desire*. She takes the English that's become staid and boring, and adds something that's new and strange and exciting. These are poems that leave a taste in your mouth, and you walk away from them thinking, what did I just read? Oh, yeah. It's the Bible."
—Matthue Roth, author, *Yom Kippur A Go-Go, Never Mind the Goldbergs, My First Kafka*

(catastrophe)

Shall I mention to Abraham what I am about to do?

Pity the angels their impossible task—

Having to say:
>   Leave the city, your only one, the one that you love,
>   with its taxi stops and north wind, butcher shops
>   and wash hanging on the line.

Having to say:
>   Take hold of your sons & daughters, your reluctant
>   spouse.

Having to be believed.

There's no escaping it. Each of us may be called on
at any moment to serve this way, messenger for a message
we're unsure of.

See, behind you, a phone dangling off the hook, glass jar
tipped open on its side.

Wild boars roam freely, lapping salt wherever they find it.

The sky is crimson, the stench of bodies floods the soft
earth, but here we remain in the midst of our 10-fold
bargaining, the last to see what is already foreseen.

Surely God in heaven could have come in person to advise.
>   *(Don't look—)*

Pity the message its compulsion to be heard, its bone
white lament:
>   Why do you set yourself against me?

We Who Desire

❧

And he (Abraham) sent her (Hagar) away.

Perhaps she heard it wrong—

No way will she and the boy be thrust out, not now,
not this soon, with only some bread & a skin of water.

Perhaps she stretches out her hand:
       Will you really deliver us to the barren desert?

Or intones his name over and over, sobbing
like the last woman on Earth.

Pity the story its need to move forward:
       Its devotion to conclusion, the ruthless pace
       of anguish.

See the small tribe of man woman boy enacting
a present etched in black fire.

Imagine the dialogue within—

       (No.) (No.) (No.)

❧

Take your son, your favored one…

Pity survivors their providence—

Having to say:
       Once I had faith servitude would serve me.

Having to say:
       Once I gathered up firestone and twig gladly,

Sue Swartz

but what has come to pass has caught me
up short.

Having to look back.

Each of us may be called upon. See behind you—

A boy, mute, favored son of a jealous mother.
Some wood. Ram roasting on a spit.

The story enters without mercy. Surely God in heaven
could have come in person to say.
       (One can live without having survived—)

Pity. Pity all around.

ANATOMY OF THE THIGH

And Jacob wrestled with the angel until dawn—

What does the human thigh know?

Muscle, fascia, and blood, inguinal ligament,
saphenous vein; stretch of plié, ache
for the lover's caress.

It should not, is not
meant to know
the sear of flaming gasoline
tendons ripped apart by wire
or common nails blown deep into the tenderness
of a young woman, nails
which in another time might be used
for the floorboards of a new start,
her leg which in another time
might feel the brush of flimsy skirt,
her name exploded into history
on the Number 18
Egged bus.

If the thigh asked for a bite of our shining apple,
would we comply, knowing
that after the first burst of red
our wild-eyed romance with death
would be laid bare?

How could we stand to say:
  You who were innocent at dawn
  shall be no more.

How could we stand to say:
  This shambling sorrow, too,
  is a blessing.

Sue Swartz

(and this desire as well)

Rightly speak the daughters of Zeloph'had!

Deep in the wandering come the daughters of Zeloph'had.
They stand before Moses   & the High Priest
before the gray-haired Elders   & the entire community

and do not flinch. They bring
no theory   no dogma   no theology

Only the hum of uncertainty—
> *Why should our father's land be lost to us*
> *and all who come after just because*
> *there is no son?*

They rise before all Israel   before all history
to say give us a holding. On razor thin circumstance
these daughters balance, they and all their descendants—

union maids   women's libbers   grrrl gangs
& the one who says *you can make your own damned dinner,*
I'm going out with the girls.

All of them and all of us   all of theirs & all of ours
perch before the Holy Tent   before the Elders.

We stand and do not flinch   but wait.
Wait for a God we can believe in.

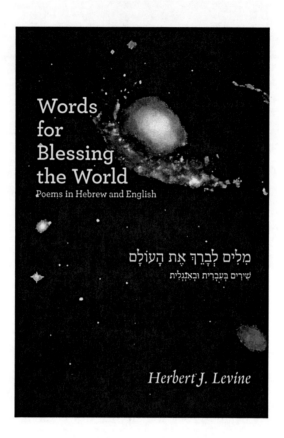

"Herbert Levine's poems build a precious bridge across the secular-religious gap in Jewish life with top-of-the-line intellectual and spiritual building materials. His work engrosses, exalts, and amuses me all at the same time, bringing me to many of the ah-ha! moments that liturgy and poetry, at their best, can evoke."
—**Lawrence Bush,** editor, *Jewish Currents*

"A learned and sincere engagement with Jewish tradition. The author suggests that we can pray 'in a world without a master.' The poems express a faith that is committed to human evolution toward more compassion, love, unity and justice. The poems are resonant with Biblical poetry and story. The Hebrew is elegant and prayerful. A gracious and powerful spiritual tool for our time."
—**Rabbi Sheila Peltz Weinberg**, author, *God Loves the Stranger: Stories, Poems and Prayers*

Herbert J. Levinie

This is the Torah

This is the Torah
that was written by human beings
over many generations
that Ezra put before the people of Israel
in the name of Moses
that Hillel the elder summarized
hundreds of years after Ezra:
What is hateful to you, don't do to your fellow.
The rest is commentary that's worth studying
and, afterwards, do what needs doing.

Our ancestors were right when they said that one mitzvah
leads to another and, likewise, a misdeed.
This I know from the mistakes of my life.
I don't believe in a commander, but the language of
"Thou shalt" reminds me that we inherited
the mitzvot in order to be refined,
like silver in the hands of the smith,
like gold separated from its dross.

I Believe with Perfect Faith

I believe with perfect faith
that the Jews came out of Egypt to testify
that there are narrow straits in every place
that all of us must pass through
to march toward a promised land
that we will not reach,
but which will never disappear from our eyes

Herbert J. Levinie

About the author

Maxine Silverman is the author of *Palimpsest* (Dos Madres Press) and four chapbooks: *Survival Song, Red Delicious* (in *Desire Path*, the inaugural volume in the Quartet Series from toadlily press), *52 Ways of Looking*, and *Transport of the Aim*, a garland of poems on the lives of Emily Dickinson, Thomas Wentworth Higginson and Celia Thaxter. Winner of a Pushcart Prize and honorable mention for Nimrod/ Pablo Neruda Prize for Poetry, she has published poems and essays in journals (among them *Lillith, Natural Bridge, Nimrod* and *you are here: the journal of creative geography*), anthologies (including *Voices from the Ark: the New Jewish Poets* and *Pushcart Prize III*), and Enskyment: Online Archive of American Poetry. "Life List" is inscribed on granite at Edmands Park in Newton, MA —her most unusual publication thus far.

A native of Sedalia, MO, she now lives in Nyack-on-Hudson, NY, with her husband and garden. They are parents of two grown sons. In addition to poetry, she creates collage, bricolage and visual midrash. Her website is www.maxinegsilverman.com.

CPSIA information can be obtained
at www.ICGtesting.com
Printed in the USA
FFOW05n2233201217